D0852389

STEM *trailblazer* BIOS

ENVIRONMENTALIST
RACHEL CARSON

DOUGLAS HUSTAD

Lerner Publications ◆ Minneapolis

Lerner Publications Company
A division of Lerner Publishing Group, Inc.
241 First Avenue North
Minneapolis, MN 55401 U.S.A.

For reading levels and more information, look up this title at www.lernerbooks.com.

Content Consultant: Dr. Patricia DeMarco, Senior Scholar, Chatham University

Library of Congress Cataloging-in-Publication Data

Names: Hustad, Douglas, author.
Title: Environmentalist Rachel Carson / by Douglas Hustad.
Description: Minneapolis : Lerner Publications, [2016] | Series: STEM trailblazer bios | Includes
    bibliographical references and index. | Audience: Ages 7–11.
Identifiers: LCCN 2015048782 (print) | LCCN 2015049189 (ebook) | ISBN 9781512407877 (library
    binding : alk. paper) | ISBN 9781512413120 (pbk. : alk. paper) | ISBN 9781512410907 (eb pdf)
Subjects: LCSH: Carson, Rachel, 1907–1964—Juvenile literature. | Carson, Rachel, 1907–1964.
    Silent spring—Juvenile literature. | Naturalists—United States—Biography—Juvenile literature.
    | Environmentalists—United States—Biography—Juvenile literature. | Science writers—United
    States—Biography—Juvenile literature. | Pesticides—Environmental aspects—Juvenile literature.
Classification: LCC QH91.3.C3 H87 2016 (print) | LCC QH91.3.C3 (ebook) | DDC 508.092—dc23

LC record available at http://lccn.loc.gov/2015048782

Manufactured in the United States of America
1 – PC – 7/15/16

CONTENTS

Chapter 1

Rachel Carson reads to her dog, Candy, near her home in Pennsylvania.

AN EYE FOR DETAIL

Rachel Carson's childhood home was the ideal place for a girl who loved science. Her family's farm in rural Pennsylvania was 65 acres (26 hectares) of forests and streams. As a girl, she loved to explore these places.

EXPLORING NATURE

Rachel's mother taught her to appreciate nature and to learn all about it. When exploring her world, Rachel had a unique eye for detail. She noticed all of the plants and animals in the woods. Rachel particularly liked to watch for birds. She loved the thrill of discovery. Once, Rachel found a **fossil** of a fish on the cliffs behind the family's farm. Right away, she wondered where it had come from and what had caused the fossil to form. She did not yet have the tools to answer these questions. But finding the fossil inspired her to learn.

RACHEL THE WRITER

Two of Rachel's biggest passions were reading and writing. She loved the books of Beatrix Potter. She also wrote her own stories and illustrated them with her drawings. At the age of ten, one of her stories was published in a children's magazine.

Rachel was an excellent student. She graduated at the top of her high school class. Graduating seniors were required to write an essay. Rachel wrote hers about the importance of education and hard work. She believed that an education did not stop outside the classroom. It continued through reading books and observing the outside world.

STUDYING BIOLOGY

Carson went on to the Pennsylvania College for Women. She first studied English. Although she had always been interested in science, she did not intend to study it in college. However, her plans changed when she was required to take a course in **biology**. The subject soon became her passion. She graduated with a biology degree in 1929.

To pay for graduate school, Carson started working part-time in a biology lab. She also taught in the **zoology** department at the University of Maryland. In the summer, she worked at the Woods Hole **Oceanographic** Institution where

Carson did zoology research aboard a sample-collecting vessel at Woods Hole, Massachusetts, in 1929.

she learned a lot about the sea. She earned a master's degree in zoology from Johns Hopkins University in 1932.

Carson wanted to pursue a **doctorate** degree. However, she could not afford it. Her father had recently passed away, and that stretched the family's budget. She also had to take care of her aging mother. Instead of pursuing her doctorate, Carson sought full-time work.

Chapter 2

Carson watches migrating hawks at Hawk Mountain, Pennsylvania, in 1945.

STUDYING THE SEA

In 1935, Carson's career as a scientist began with a writing assignment. She was hired by the United States Bureau of Fisheries to write scripts for a radio series about marine life. The following year they hired Carson as a junior aquatic

biologist. One of her projects was to study how the fishing industry in Chesapeake Bay affected fish populations.

WRITING ABOUT THE SEA

While working for the Bureau of Fisheries, Carson also did her own independent research and writing about sea life. In 1937 she published an article in *Atlantic Monthly* magazine, called "Undersea." It described a colorful journey along the ocean floor. Carson was good at describing scientific details in a way that could be understood by readers who were not scientists. The article was the basis for her first book, *Under the Sea-Wind*, published in 1941.

In *Under the Sea-Wind*, Carson wrote about animals living in and near the ocean. One species she wrote about was the sanderling shore bird.

Carson hikes with the Audubon Naturalist Society on Cobb Island, Virginia, in 1947.

Carson's book described many aspects of ocean life. It explained how creatures living in and near the sea interact with each other. It also showed how they each struggle to survive. But the book came out just a few weeks before Pearl Harbor was attacked by Japan. Within days, the United States had entered World War II (1939–1945). The book's release was overshadowed by world events. It did not become as popular as Carson had hoped.

A SECOND BOOK

Carson continued to work at the Bureau of Fisheries, which had been renamed the United States Fish and Wildlife Service in 1940. In the late 1940s, Carson began to work on a second book about the sea. She wanted to write about the origins of Earth's oceans and the power of the tides. To learn more on the subject, she applied to go on a trip aboard a Woods Hole research ship traveling to the Georges Bank in the Atlantic Ocean. But officials did not like the idea of a single woman on board a ship crewed entirely by men. Her request was denied.

On a 1949 trip with a University of Miami research vessel, Carson prepares for a diving expedition.

Determined to conduct her research, Carson persuaded the Fish and Wildlife Service to allow her aboard if she brought a chaperone. She chose Marie Rodell, her literary agent. On the trip, Carson studied the deep-sea creatures that were brought up from the ocean in nets. She observed fish, crabs, starfish, and other creatures. This research generated a lot of material for her next book.

The book was published in July 1951 as *The Sea Around Us*. It was an instant success. It won awards and was on the bestseller list for eighty-six weeks. Carson left her job in 1952. She wanted to concentrate on her own research and writing. A year later, *The Sea Around Us* was made into a **documentary**. Ultimately, Carson did not like the film. She felt the director had introduced scientific errors into the work. However, the film won an Academy Award for Best Documentary in 1953.

TECH TALK

"If there is poetry in my book about the sea, it is not because I deliberately put it there, but because no one could write truthfully about the sea and leave out the poetry."

—*Rachel Carson on* The Sea Around Us

Carson (*right*) conducts marine biology research in Florida with colleague Bob Hines in 1952.

A TROUBLING OBSERVATION

In 1955, Carson published a third book, *The Edge of the Sea*. It was about the environment along the coast of the Atlantic seashore. While researching her books, Carson had discovered something startling. High levels of chemicals in the water were affecting marine life. Other scientists were noticing this disturbing trend as well. It was not an area she had planned to study. But Carson felt the issue was too important to ignore. She began to conduct more research on the impact of these chemicals.

Chapter 3

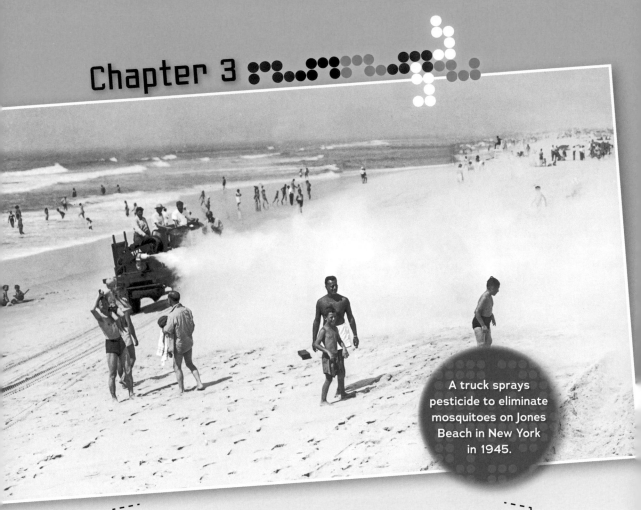

A truck sprays pesticide to eliminate mosquitoes on Jones Beach in New York in 1945.

WRITING
SILENT SPRING

In the 1950s, technology advanced quickly. Companies were using more and more chemicals to solve problems. One big problem was the insects that eat farm crops. Companies developed chemicals called pesticides to kill these insects and

improve food production. However, scientists soon discovered that these chemicals could be dangerous.

WILDLIFE IN DANGER

One of the first pesticides was called DDT. It was very effective at killing insects. But it was also killing wildlife. Carson

Scientists pump DDT into an artificial pond in 1945 to test the effects of the pesticide on larvae and fishes.

Carson did some of her writing outdoors. Here she takes notes in the woods near her home in Silver Spring, Maryland, in 1962.

had previously noticed high levels of DDT in marine life. In 1958, a friend sent Carson a letter, noting that many birds had died after government officials sprayed DDT in her area to kill mosquitoes.

Carson felt the issue needed to be publicized. She suggested that the *New Yorker* do a story on it. Its editor agreed. So Carson began working on what would become her

DDT was widely used in the United States in the 1950s.

most famous book, *Silent Spring*. The title came to her after she imagined a spring without any birdsong.

THE BEST WRITER FOR THE JOB

Fish and wildlife felt the effects of DDT first. So Carson's studies of animal populations for the Fish and Wildlife Service made her one of the best people to write the book. She spent years researching and writing *Silent Spring*. She consulted with experts in the United States and Europe. She got access to research on DDT that had not yet been made easily available to the public. One of the scientists she met was

A normal peregrine falcon egg (*left*) has a much stronger shell than one that has been poisoned by DDT (*right*).

Joseph Hickey, who worked at the University of Wisconsin. His research proved that pesticides were causing the eggshells of birds to become thin and weak. This had led to a decrease in bird populations. Carson documented all of this information carefully so it could be included in her book.

Carson studies tissue samples at her home in Silver Spring, Maryland, in 1962.

TECH TALK

"The chemical pesticides are a bright new toy. They sometimes work in a spectacular way, giving those who wield them a giddy sense of power over nature. . . . Disregarding the whole record of contamination and death, we continue to spray. . . . We proceed as if there were no alternative, even though there are alternatives."

—*Rachel Carson's essay in the June 16, 1962, issue of the* New Yorker

Carson followed all news about pesticides very closely. She attended hearings of the Food and Drug Administration (FDA), a government organization that makes sure foods in the United States are safe to eat. Fruits and vegetables treated with pesticides had been discovered to have high levels of toxic chemicals. The companies who made the pesticides had to convince the FDA they were safe. Carson took note of the techniques that chemical companies used to keep their pesticides in use. She combined all this scientific information into a story that could be easily understood by people who were not scientists.

A DANGER TO PEOPLE AND ANIMALS

Carson saw firsthand how chemicals could affect all life on Earth. She wanted to make people understand that pesticides did not only kill pests. They left behind dangerous chemicals that could make people and animals sick.

Carson consulted with other scientists, and they agreed with her. They backed up her research and encouraged her to publish. But the makers of the pesticides were huge corporations. They rushed to stop *Silent Spring* from being published, but they did not succeed.

The research and writing process took Carson several years to complete. She wanted to include as many sources as possible because she felt the book was going to be closely scrutinized. Carson also was having health problems. In 1960, she was diagnosed with cancer. But Carson worked through these challenges and finished her book two years later. The *New Yorker* published it in a series of three long articles, starting in June 1962. Then *Silent Spring* was published as a book in September 1962.

Silent Spring received both criticism and acclaim when it was released in September 1962.

Chapter 4

Because of her work on *Silent Spring*, Carson testified before a government committee studying pesticides in June 1963.

CONTROVERSIES AND CRITICISM

As soon as *Silent Spring* came out, chemical companies tried to discredit it. They not only questioned Carson's research, but also attacked her as a person and scientist.

They called her misinformed and said she knew nothing about science. Some of these criticisms were based on ignorance. People simply did not know that pesticides were dangerous.

VOCAL CRITICS

Critics claimed that the book was not scientific because there was no discussion of both sides. Carson did not list pros and cons of pesticides. But that was because to her, there were no positives. Yes, pesticides killed insects. But the cost, in her opinion, far outweighed the benefits.

Carson did not argue that pesticides should never be used. However, she made a strong case that certain pesticides, such as DDT, were damaging to people and the environment. She argued that DDT spread easily throughout an ecosystem. Its hazardous chemicals remained inside animal tissue, so it affected the entire food chain. For example, a fish might eat a plant that had absorbed toxic chemicals from the water. If the fish was then eaten by an eagle, the eagle would absorb the chemicals into its tissue as well. Animals high on the food chain would receive the highest levels of these toxins. Too many of the toxins could cause illness or death. Humans who ate food containing pesticides might face the same threat.

Reporter Eric Sevareid (*right*) interviews Carson for an episode of *CBS Reports* that aired in April 1963.

A CAUSE FOR CHANGE

The criticisms of *Silent Spring* were many. But there were also many positive reactions. Before the book came out, forty thousand copies had already been sold in advance. And after the book was available, there was a television special on it. Reviews ran in dozens of newspapers. Even President John F. Kennedy cited *Silent Spring* as a reason for the government to take a closer look at pesticides. The President's Science Advisory Committee (PSAC) was launched to examine Carson's findings.

The PSAC released its report in May 1963 after eight months of research. It found that not nearly enough was

> "All this [evidence] gives us reason to think deeply and seriously about the means by which these residues reach the places where we are now discovering them."
>
> —Rachel Carson, in her 1963 testimony to Congress

known about the negative effects of pesticides. And the report stated that without Carson, people would have remained unaware. As part of related investigations, Carson testified before Congress in June 1963. By the end of the year, most attacks on her and the book had died down. *Silent Spring* was a bestseller, and farmers scaled back the use of pesticides.

Carson's testimony was one of her last public appearances. She was losing her battle with cancer. On April 14, 1964, at the age of fifty-six, she passed away. Her funeral was held at the National Cathedral in Washington, DC, where presidents and other important Americans have been laid to rest. Many politicians came out to honor her.

A LASTING LEGACY

Carson's impact on the use of pesticides is well-known. Eight of the twelve pesticides she mentioned in *Silent Spring* were eventually banned in the United States. But Carson's most long-lasting contribution was to the environmental movement. Before *Silent Spring*, awareness of environmental impacts was minimal. People knew it was important to preserve land and take care of natural resources. But it was not well understood how human activities were doing damage to the environment.

Decades after her death, Carson's work still influences and inspires environmentalists. More than two million copies of *Silent Spring* have been sold. Carson has been given many honors. She was also named one of the one hundred most influential people of the 1900s by *Time* magazine. Through her scientific research and tireless advocacy, Carson and her work live on around the world.

TECH TALK

"It's happened many times. A book—a single book—has changed American life, changed our history. . . . The most important of all such books [is] *Silent Spring*."

—*Pulitzer Prize-winning biographer and historian David McCullough during a 1993 public television documentary on Carson*

TIMELINE

1907

Rachel Carson is born in Springdale, Pennsylvania, on May 27.

1929

Carson graduates from the Pennsylvania College for Women with a degree in biology.

1932

Carson earns her master's degree in zoology from Johns Hopkins University.

1936

Carson begins working at the United States Bureau of Fisheries.

1939

DDT is first used as a pesticide.

1945

Carson proposes an article on DDT to *Readers Digest*, but her idea is rejected.

1962

Carson finishes *Silent Spring* and it is published.

1963

The President's Science Advisory Committee issues a report confirming Carson's findings.

1964

Carson dies in Silver Spring, Maryland.

SOURCE NOTES

6   Linda Lear, *Rachel Carson: Witness for Nature* (New York: Henry Holt and Company, Inc., 1997), 24.

12 Rachel Carson, "Rachel Carson, Winner of the 1952 Nonfiction Award for *The Sea Around Us*," *National Book Awards Acceptance Speeches,* National Book Foundation, 1952, http://www.nationalbook.org/nbaacceptspeech_rcarson .html#.Vk4Yqd-rS3c.

18 Rachel Carson and Dorothy Freeman, *Always, Rachel: The Letters of Rachel Carson and Dorothy Freeman, 1952–1964—The Story of a Remarkable Friendship*, ed. Martha Freeman (Boston: Beacon Press, 1996), xxvii.

21 Rachel Carson, "Silent Spring—I," *New Yorker* (June 16, 1962): 99.

27 "Rachel Carson testifies to Ribicoff Committee," ITN Source, http://www .itnsource.com/shotlist/BHC_FoxMovietone/1963/06/05/X05066302/#3.

28 "Rachel Carson's *Silent Spring*," *American Experience*, aired 1993 (Arlington, VA: PBS, 2007), DVD.

GLOSSARY

biology
the study of living things

doctorate
a degree earned after a bachelor's and a master's

documentary
a movie or television program about real people and events

fossils
bones, shells, or other parts of an animal or plant, preserved as rock

oceanography
the study of the ocean

zoology
the study of animals

FURTHER INFORMATION

BOOKS

Fabiny, Sarah. *Who Was Rachel Carson?* New York: Grosset & Dunlap, 2014. Learn more about Carson's life and work.

Lawlor, Laurie. *Rachel Carson and Her Book That Changed the World.* New York: Holiday House, 2014. Read about Carson's most important book, *Silent Spring.*

Venezia, Mike. *Rachel Carson: Clearing the Way for Environmental Protection.* New York: Scholastic, 2010. Explore Carson's lasting impact on the environmental movement.

WEBSITES

The Life and Legacy of Rachel Carson
http://www.rachelcarson.org
Go inside the life of Rachel Carson and discover more resources to learn about her work.

Natural Resources Defense Council: The Story of *Silent Spring*
http://www.nrdc.org/health/pesticides/hcarson.asp
Go even further in depth with the story of *Silent Spring* and its impact.

The Rachel Carson Council
http://www.rachelcarsoncouncil.org/index.php
See the current environmental challenges facing the world and find out what you can do to help.

LERNER
SOURCE

Expand learning beyond the printed book. Download free, complementary educational resources for this book from our website, www.lerneresource.com.

INDEX

ABOUT THE AUTHOR

Douglas Hustad is a children's author who has written several books on science and technology for young people. Originally from northern Minnesota, he now lives in San Francisco with his wife.